Festival Knits 2

Festival Knits Volume 2: More One Skein Projects Featuring Indie Dyers

ISBN 13 (print): 978-1-937513-98-6

First edition

Published by http://www.cooperativepress.com

Patterns, charts ©2022 Shannon Okey

Photos ©2022 Shannon Okey

Models: Candra Squire, Shannon Okey

Senior Technical Editor: Andi Smith

Book layout: Kim Saar with special thanks to Emily Kuhn for cover logotype.

Sample knitters: Sarah Jo Burch, Jessy Needles, Amy Ross Phillips Manko, Kim Saar, Shannon Saar, Cadence Fingerholz, Candace Musmeci, Marie Duquette, Stephanie McGuckin

Every effort has been made to ensure that all the information in this book is accurate at the time of publication; however, Cooperative Press neither endorses nor guarantees the content of external links referenced in this book.

If you have questions or comments about this book, or need information about licensing, custom editions, special sales, or academic/corporate purchases, please contact Cooperative Press: info@cooperativepress.com or 10252 Berea Rd, Cleveland, Ohio 44102 USA

No part of this book may be reproduced in any form, except brief excerpts for the purpose of review, without prior written permission of the publisher. Thank you for respecting our copyright.

Festival Knits 2

More one skein projects featuring indie dyers

Cooperative Press
Cleveland, Ohio

Patterns

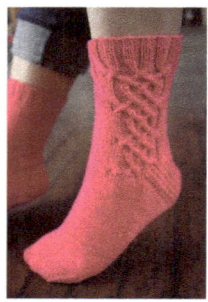
Beacon, 6

Fishkill, 12

Chelsea, 16

Mulberry, 20

Tivoli, 24

Kalina, 30

Amenia, 34

Verbank, 38

Wynkoop, 42

Intro

Let's talk about community. This book was brought to life in order to show off the beautiful yarns my friends/colleagues make. We specifically chose dyers who would be at New York State Sheep and Wool Festival in 2022, the second year the event will held in person since the start of the pandemic, and we targeted the book release to have it available for sale there.

My genius tech editor Andi Smith worked her usual magic on the patterns and charts in this book, and we hired a team of sample knitters to bring the designs to life quickly. Sample knitters are the unsung heroes of the knit design industry, and don't get nearly enough pay or credit for all their hard work! Believe me, I would be lost without them. I'm a slower knitter than I would like to be, and a better project manager, honestly. With that in mind, we put this book together in such a way as to optimize everyone's talents and to celebrate this community of ours.

Over the past almost we have seen the knitting community respond to the worldwide COVID pandemic with the kind of creative, think-on-your-feet skills knitters are known for, and the 2020 Maryland festival really stands out to me as one amazing example. A show that takes months and months to organize was put online in less than six weeks. We pulled two books from our archives (*Doomsday Knits* and *Subversive Socks*) that had gone out of print and printed a limited run of new copies to preorder "at" Maryland. *Doomsday* ended up in the New York Times, of all places, and I spent much of that summer filling orders for it. Frankly, it saved us financially in a year when so many events canceled. The small businesses that make up much of the online knitting community pulled together to help cross promote each other and keep spirits high. (Keep in mind most of these businesses are one, maybe two people tops behind the scenes). And many new knitters got their start during lockdowns! It's been a wild two years, and I have never been happier to be a part of this worldwide community of creative people. I hope you'll enjoy these patterns and check out the dyers who made the beautiful yarns.

Beacon

Required Skills
Working in the round

Cables

Picking up stitches

Grafting

Sizes
S (M, L)

Finished Measurements
8 (9, 10) inches / 20.25 (22.75, 25.5) cm

intended to be worn with .5 to 1 inch of negative ease.

Materials
Neighborhood Fiber Co. Organic Studio Sock (100% Organic Merino; 400yds / 365m per 4oz / 113g skein); color: Mondawmin: 1 skein

US#2 / 2.75 mm needles configured for small circumference circular knitting

Cable needle

Stitch marker

Yarn needle

Gauge
32 sts x 40 rnds = 4 inches / 10 cm in stitch pattern, unstretched

Pattern Notes
This sock is worked from the cuff down, with the cable detail running down the outside of the leg to the ankle.

After the 2 x 2 rib, Chart A is worked once, followed by repeats of Chart B, then has a heel flap, turn, gusset construction.

This pattern is written assuming the knitter is working on two circular needles.

Stitches and Techniques

cn	cable needle
k	knit
k2tog	knit 2 sts together
p	purl
p2tog	purl 2 sts together
rnd(s)	round(s)
sl	slip (purlwise, unless otherwise stated)
st(s)	stitch(es)
ssk	slip, slip, knit the two slipped sts together through the back loop
2/2 LC	slip 2 sts to cn, hold in front, k2, k2 from cn
2/2 LpC	slip 2 sts to cn, hold in front, p2, k2 from cn
2/2 RC	slip 2 sts to cn, hold in back, k2, k2 from cn
2/2 RpC	slip 2 sts to cn, hold in back, k2, p2 from cn

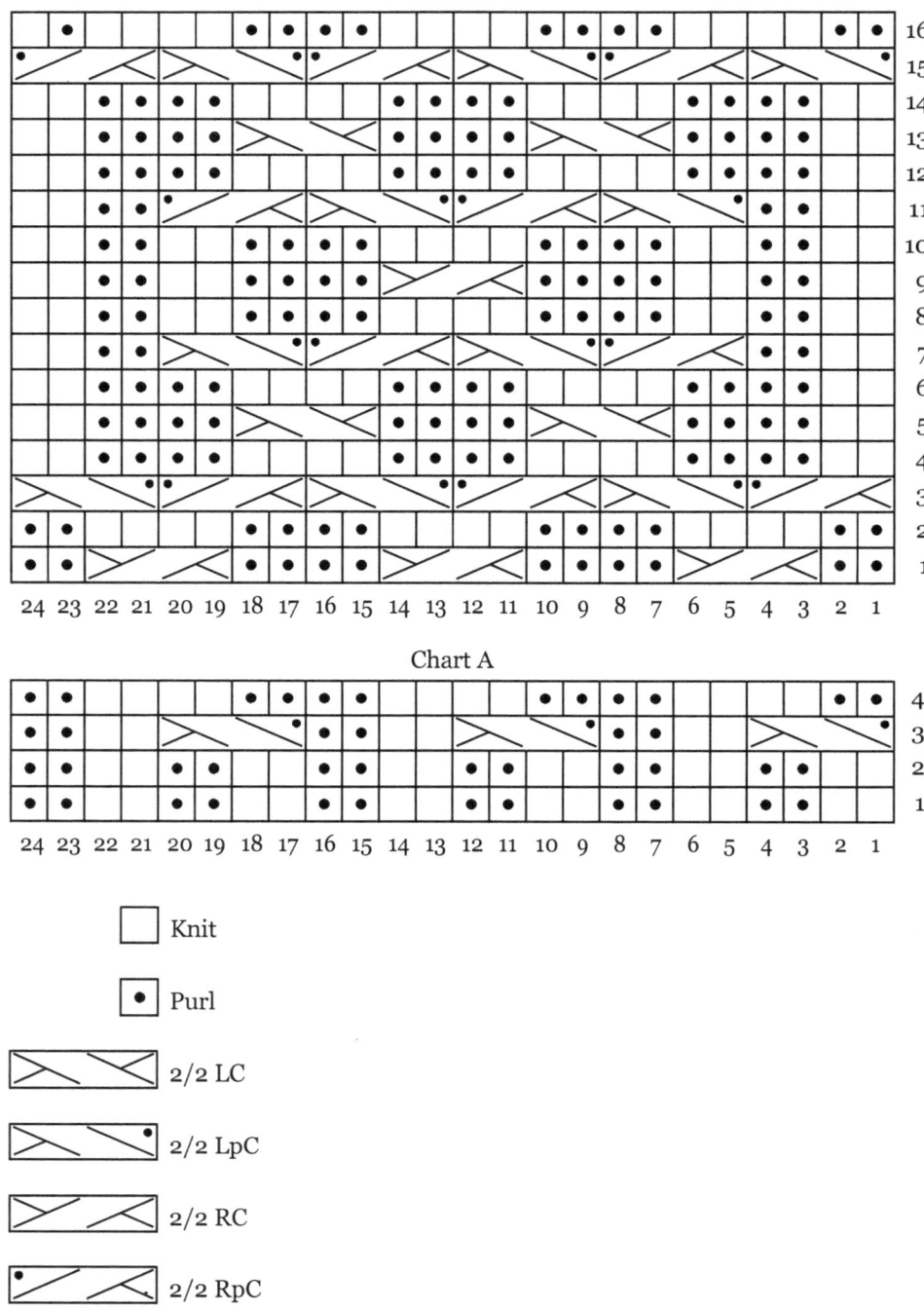

Pattern

Cuff

Using German Twisted, or your favorite stretchy method, cast on 64 (72, 80) sts. Join to work in the round, placing a marker to denote the beginning of the round.

Rnd 1: *K2, p2; repeat from * to end of rnd.

Work 10 (14, 18) repeats of Rnd 1.

Work first rnd of Chart A across the first 24 sts, then in pattern as established across the rest of the rnd.

Work the remaining rnds of Chart A across the first 24 sts, keeping the remaining sts as established.

Leg

Work the 16 rnds of Chart B over the first 24 sts, and knit the remaining sts over each rnd, until sock measures 6 (6.5, 7) inches / 15.25 (16.5, 17.75), or your desired length. Break yarn.

Heel divide

Move the first 12 sts to the end of the last rnd.

Now arrange your sts so that the rnd is divided in half – 32 (36, 40) sts on each needle.

Left Leg

Working on the needle that has the yarn break, work the heel as follows:

Right Leg

Working on needle that doesn't have the yarn break, work the heel as follows:

Heel

Row 1: *K1tbl, p1; repeat for a total of 32 (36, 40) sts. Turn.

Row 2: Slip 1, purl. Turn

Repeat these 2 rows for a total of 17 (19, 21) times.

Heel turn

Row 1: K1, k17 (19, 21), ssk, k1. Turn.

Row 2: Sl1, p5, p2tog, p1. Turn.

Row 3: Sl1, knit to 1 st before the gap, ssk, k1. Turn.

Row 4: Sl1, p to 1 st before the gap, p2tog, p1. Turn.

Work repeats of Rows 3 and 4 until all the heel sts have been incorporated.

Gusset

Knit across the heel turn sts, pick up and knit 17 (19, 21) sts along the heel, work in St. st across the remaining 32 (36, 40) sts, then pick up and knit 17 (19, 21) sts down the other side of the heel.

Break yarn, and arrange your sts so that the 32 (36, 40) front of sock sts are on the first needle, and the remaining heel sts are on the second needle.

Rnd 1: Knit.

Rnd 2: Knit across first needle, k1, ssk, k to last 3 sts, k2tog, k1.

Work repeats of Rnds 1 and 2 until your second needle has decreased to 32 (36, 40) sts.

Foot

Work without shaping until, when tried on, the sock is 2 (2.25, 2.5) inches / 5 (5.75, 6.25) cm shorter than desired length.

Toe

Rnd 1: [K1, ssk, k to 3 sts before end of needle, k2tog, k1] twice.

Rnd 2: Knit.

Work repeats of Rnds 1 and 2 until you have 16 (18, 20) sts remaining on each needle.

Break yarn, leaving a long tail. Graft the sts closed, using a seamless grafting technique.

Finishing

Weave in all ends securely, and block following the ball band instructions.

Fishkill

Required Skills

Working in the round

Increases / decreases

Simple lace from chart

Grafting

Sizes

M (L)

Finished Measurements

Cirucmference 9 (10) inches / 22.75, (25.5) cm - intended to be worn with .5 to 1 inch / 1.25 to 2.5 cm of negative ease.

Materials

Miss Babs Katahdin 437 (100% Superwash BFL; 437yds / 400m per 3.5oz / 99g skein); color: Babette/Heading Home: 1 skein -

US#2 / 2.75 mm circular needles

Stitch marker

waste yarn, or stitch holder for afterthought heel

Yarn needle

Gauge

32 sts x 40 rnds = 4 inches / 10 cm in stitch pattern, unstretched

Pattern Notes

This sock is worked from the top down, and has an afterthought heel.

Stitches and Techniques Abbreviations

CDD	(central double decrease) sl1, k2tog, psso
k	knit
k2tog	knit 2 sts together
p	purl
rnd(s)	round(s)
st(s)	stitch(es)
ssk	slip, slip, knit the two slipped sts together through the back loop
yo	yarn over

The sock has a rib, then lace across the leg, and front of foot.

Pattern

Cuff

Using your favorite stretchy method, cast on 72 (84) sts, and join to work in the round, placing a stitch marker at the beginning of the round, dividing the sts so that you have 36 (42) sts on each of two needles

Rnd 1: *P1, k1; repeat from * to end of rnd.

Repeat Rnd 1 for 1.5 (2) inches / 3.75

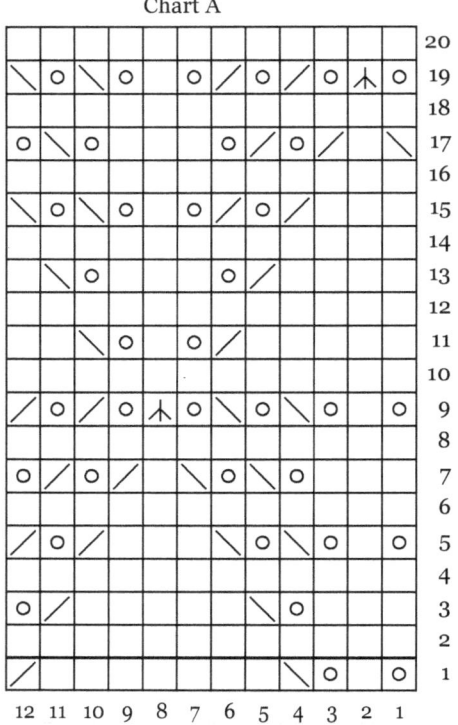

Chart A

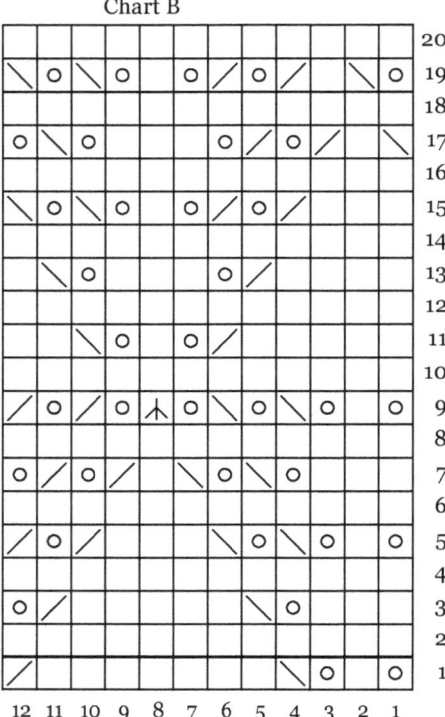

Chart B

(5) cm.

Leg

Work repeats of the 16 rnds of the chart across all sts, until your sock measures 6 (7) inches / 15.25 (17.75) cm, or your desired length, ending after Rnd 20.

NOTE On Rnd 19 - slip the first st to RH needle to start the rnd to align the sts.

Afterthought heel prep rnd

With waste yarn, knit across the first needle, leaving a 6 inch / 15.25cm tail on either side of the sts.

Slide the sts back to the beginning of the needle, and reknit them with working yarn, knit across the remaining sts.

Foot

Size M: Work Chart B three times across front of sock

Size L: K3, work Chart B three times across front of sock, k3

Both sizes

Knit across bottom of sock, and work Chart B as placed above across front of sock until your foot measures 1.5 (2) inches / 3.75 (5) cm shorter than your foot.

Toe

Rnd 1: Knit.

Rnd 2: [K1, ssk, k to 3 sts before end of needle, k2tog, k1] twice.

Repeat Rnds 1 and 2 until you have 18 (20) sts on each needle.

Break the yarn. Graft sts together using your favorite seamless technique.

Afterthought heel

Working from one side of your heel prep rnd, carefully remove the waste yarn, a couple of sts at a time, placing the lower sts onto one needle, and the upper sts onto the second needle.

Make sure to count your sts, and ensure that you have the same number – if the number is off by one, work a k2tog at the beginning of the next rnd if necessary.

Rnd 1: Knit.

Rnd 2: [K1, ssk, k to 3 sts before end of needle, k2tog, k1] twice.

Repeat Rnds 1 and 2 until you have 18 (20) sts on each needle.

Break the yarn. Graft sts together using your favorite seamless technique.

Finishing

Weave in all ends. Block according to your ball band instructions.

Chelsea

Required Skills
Working in the round

Increases / decreases

Simple lace from chart

Sizes
S (M, L)

Finished Measurements
Circumference 8.5 (9.5, 10.5) inches / 21.5 (24, 26.75) cm – unstretched

Materials
Ross Farms (100% Leicester Longwool; 250yds / 223m per 140g skein); color: Natural: 2 skeins

US#6 / 10 mm circular needles

Stitch marker

Yarn needle

Gauge
10 sts x 32 rnds = 4 inches / 10 cm in pattern, unstretched

Stitches and Techniques
k	knit
k3tog	knit 3 sts together
ktbl	knit through the back loop
p	purl
rnd(s)	round(s)
row(s)	row(s)
st(s)	stitch(es)
ssk	slip, slip, knit the two slipped sts together through the back loop
Sssk	slip, slip, slip, knit the three slipped through the back loop
yo	yarn over

Pattern notes

This leg warmer is worked from the bottom up.

Pattern

Cuff

Using your favorite stretchy method, cast on 56 (70, 84) sts. Join to work in the round, placing a marker to denote the beginning of the round.

Rnd 1: *K1tbl, p1; repeat from * to end of rnd.

Work repeats of Rnd 1 until cuff measures 2 (2.25, 2.5) inches / 5 (5.75, 6.25) cm in depth.

Leg

Work the 14 sts of the chart across the rnd, and then repeats of all 16 rnds, until your leg warmer measures 12 (13, 14) inches / 30.5 (33, 35.5) cm, from the start, ending after a 16th rnd.

Top cuff

Rnd 1: *K1tbl, p1; repeat from * to end of rnd.

Work repeats of Rnd 1 until cuff measures 2 (2.25, 2.5) inches / 5 (5.75, 6.25) cm in depth.

Finishing

Weave in ends. Block according to your ball band instructions.

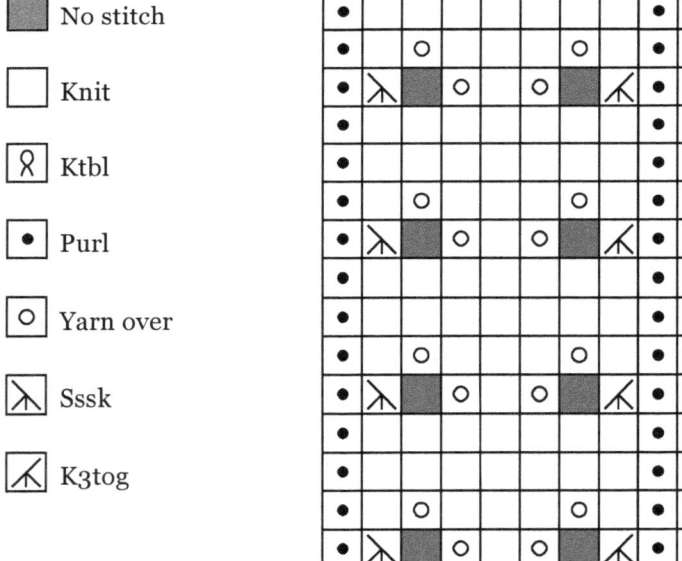

Mulberry

Required Skills

Working in the round

Increases / decreases

Colorwork

Grafting

Sizes

S (M, L)

Finished Measurements

Circumference 7 (8.5, 9.5) inches / 17.75 (21.5, 22.75) cm – unstretched

Materials

Dragonfly Fibers Dragon Sock (100% superwash Merino; 390yds / 356m per 4oz / 113g skein); color: Mr Carson: 1 skein

Dragonfly Fibers Dragon Sock (100% superwash Merino; 390yds / 356m per 4oz / 113g skein); color: Saffron: 1 skein

US#2 / 2.75 mm circular needles

Stitch marker

Waste yarn for afterthought heel

Yarn needle

Gauge

32 sts x 32 rnds = 4 inches / 10 cm in pattern, unstretched

Stitches and Techniques

- **k** knit
- **k2tog** knit 2 sts together
- **ktbl** knit through the back loop
- **p** purl
- **rnd(s)** round(s)
- **row(s)** row(s)
- **st(s)** stitch(es)
- **ssk** slip, slip, knit the two slipped sts together through the back loop

Pattern notes

This is a top down, colorwork sock, with an afterthought heel.

Pattern

Cuff

With MC, and using your favorite stretchy method, cast on 60 (80, 100) sts. Divide the sts evenly over two needles and join to work in the round, placing a marker to denote the beginning of the round.

Rnd 1: *P1, k1tbl; repeat from * to end of rnd.

Work repeats of Rnd 1 for 2 (2.25, 2.5) inches / 5 (5.75, 6.25) cm.

Leg

Work repeats of Chart A across all sts, until your sock measures 8 (9, 10) inches - or your desired length - ending after Rnd 9 of the chart.

NOTE you don't have to break your CC yarn here

Afterthought heel prep

Needle 1: Work in pattern as set.

Needle 2: Knit the sts with waste yarn, leaving a 6 inch / 15.25 cm tail on either side of the sts, slide the sts back to the beginning of the needle, and reknit them with working yarn, knit across the remaining sts.

Foot

Work Chart A across first needle, and Chart B across second needle.

NOTE If you didn't end with Rnd 9

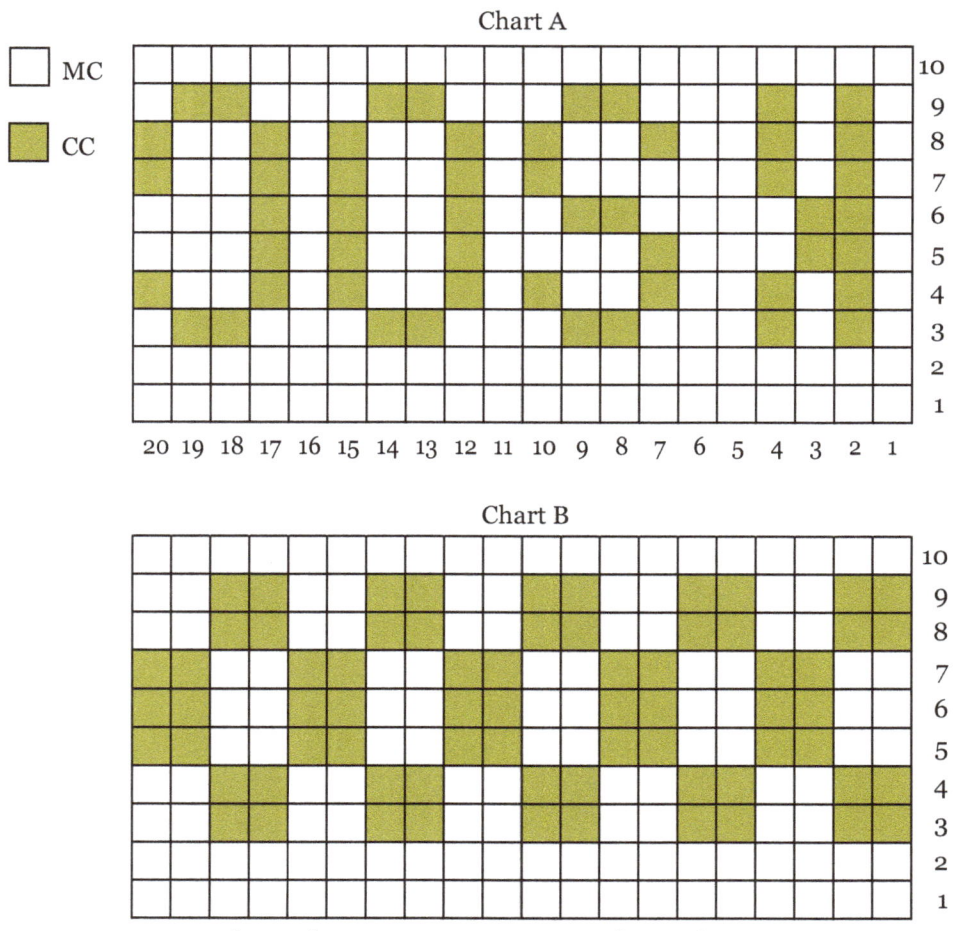

at the afterthought heel prep rnd, work Chart B from the same round number as Chart A that you're on.

Work foot until the sock is 2 (2.25, 2.5) inches / 5 (5.75, 6.25) cm shorter than your foot, ending after Rnd 10.

Toe

Rnd 1: [K1, ssk, k to 3 sts before end of needle, k2tog, k1] twice.

Rnd 2: Knit.

Repeat Rnds 1 and 2 until you have 24 (32, 44) sts on each needle.

Break yarn, leaving a long tail.

Graft the toe together using Kitchener stitch.

Afterthought heel

Working from one side of your heel prep rnd, carefully remove the waste yarn, a couple of sts at a time, placing the lower sts onto one needle, and the upper sts onto the second needle.

Make sure to count your sts, and ensure that you have the same number – if the number is off by one, work a k2tog at the beginning of the next rnd if necessary.

Rnd 1: Knit.

Rnd 2: [K1, ssk, k to 3 sts before end of needle, k2tog, k1] twice.

Repeat Rnds 1 and 2 until you have 24 (32, 44) sts on each needle.

Break the yarn. Graft your sts together using your preferred seamless grafting technique.

Finishing

Weave in ends. Block according to your ball band instructions.

Tivoli

Required Skills
Working in the round
Increases / decreases
Simple lace and cables from chart
Wrapped stitches
Grafting

Sizes
S (M, L)

Finished Measurements
Circumference 5 (6.5, 7.5) inches / 12.75 (16.5, 17.75) cm - unstretched

Materials
Fiber Optic Unified Gradients (80% Superwash Merino / 10% Cashmere / 10% Ultrafine Nylon; 255yds / 233m per 2.3oz / 65g skein); color: Texas Bluebonnet here, also seen in Stormy Weather on the cover, 2 skeins

US#2 / 2.75 mm circular needles

Cable needle

Stitch marker

Yarn needle

Gauge
24 sts x 32 rounds = 4 inches / 10 cm unstretched

Stitches and Techniques

cn	cable needle
k	knit
k2tog	knit 2 sts together
ktbl	knit through the back loop
LH	left hand
p	purl
RH	right hand
rnd(s)	round(s)
row(s)	row(s)
st(s)	stitch(es)
ssk	slip, slip, knit the two slipped sts together through the back loop
yo	yarn over
wyib	with yarn in back
wyif	with yarn in front
3 st wrap	[wyib, slip 3 sts to RH needle, wyif, slip sts back to LH needle] three times, k1, p1, k1
4 st wrap	[wyib, slip 4 sts to RH needle, wyif, slip sts back to LH needle] three times, k4
2/1 LpC	slip 2 sts to cn, hold in front, p1, k2 from cn
2/1 RpC	slip 1 st to cn, hold in back, k2, p1 from cn

2/2 LC slip 2 to cn, hold in front, k2, k2 from cn

2/2 RC slip 2 to cn, hold in back, k2, k2 from cn

3/2 LC slip 3 to cn, hold in front, k2, k3 from cn

3/2 RC slip 2 sts to cn, hold in back, k3, k2 from cn

Pattern Notes

This sock is worked from the top down, and features a gusseted heel.

It has three sizes: follow within the green lines for size S, the blue lines for size M, and the red lines for size L.

Pattern

Cuff

Using your favorite stretchy method, cast on 66 (74, 82) sts, and divide them equally on two needles. Join to work in the round, and add a stitch marker to denote the beginning of the round.

Work repeats of Chart A for 2 inches/ 5 cm.

Leg

Work Chart B twice - 48 rnds.

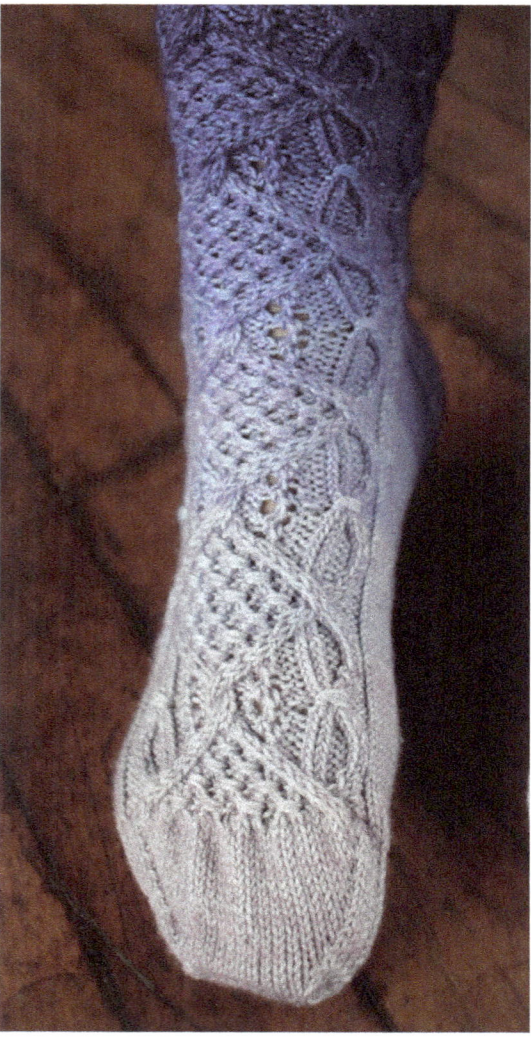

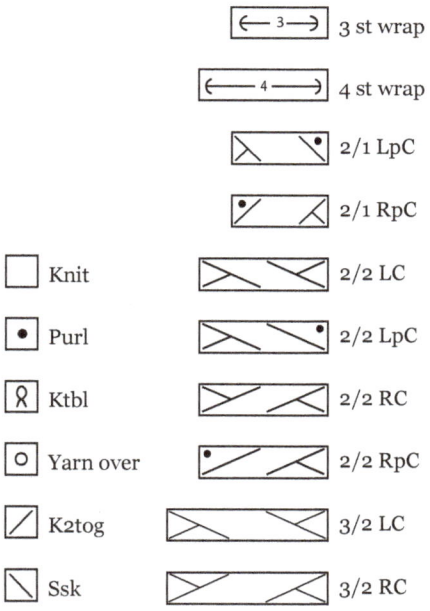

Chart A

Chart B

Large
Medium
Small

Heel

Rnd 1: Work Chart B across first needle; k2tog, k to end of second needle – 32 (36, 40) sts on second needle. Turn.

NOTE you will be working on the second needle only.

Row 2: Sl1, purl across needle. Turn.

Row 3: *Sl1, k1; repeat from * to end of row. Turn

Row 4: Sl1, purl. Turn.

Repeat Rows 3 and 4 for a total of 16 (18, 20) times.

Heel turn

Row 1: K1, k17 (19, 21), ssk, k1. Turn.

Row 2: Sl1, p5, p2tog, p1. Turn.

Row 3: Sl1, knit to 1 st before the gap, ssk, k1. Turn.

Row 4: Sl1, p to 1 st before the gap, p2tog, p1. Turn.

Work repeats of Rows 3 and 4 until all the heel sts have been incorporated.

Gusset

Knit across the heel turn sts, pick up and knit 17 (19, 21) sts along the heel, work in St. st across the remaining 33 (37, 41) sts, then pick up and knit 17 (19, 21) sts down the other side of the heel.

Break yarn, and arrange your sts so that the 33 (37, 41) front of sock sts are on the first needle, and the remaining heel sts are on the second needle.

Rnd 1: Work in pattern as established across first needle, knit across second needle.

Rnd 2: Work in pattern as established across first needle, k1, ssk, k to last 3 sts, k2tog, k1.

Work repeats of Rnds 1 and 2 until your second needle has decreased to 32 (36, 40) sts.

Foot

Work without shaping until, when tried on, the sock is 2 (2.25, 2.5) inches / 5 (5.75, 6.25) cm shorter than desired length, increasing one st across the second needle on the last rnd – 33 (37, 41) sts on each needle.

Toe

Rnd 1: [K1, ssk, k to 3 sts before end of needle, k2tog, k1] twice.

Rnd 2: Knit.

Work repeats of Rnds 1 and 2 until you have 13 (15, 17) sts remaining on each needle.

Break yarn, leaving a long tail.

Graft your sts together, using your favorite grafting technique.

Finishing

Weave in ends securely. Block according to your ball band instructions.

Kalina

Required Skills

Working in the round

Increases / decreases

Simple lace from chart

Grafting

Sizes

S (M, L)

Finished Measurements

8 (9, 10) inches / 20.25 (22.75, 25.5) cm

Materials

Loop Fiber Studio Yin Yang Fingering (100% Rambouillet; 400yds / 457m per 4oz / 100g skein); color: Far: 1 skein

US#2/ 2.75 mm circular needles, or size needed to obtain gauge

Stitch marker

Yarn needle

Waste yarn for afterthought heel

Gauge

36 sts x 40 rnds = 4 inches / 10 cm, unstretched

Stitches and Techniques

k	knit
ktbl	knit through the back loop
p	purl
rnd(s)	round(s)
row(s)	row(s)
st(s)	stitch(es)
yo	yarn over
sl1, k2tog, psso	slip 1st, k2tog, pass slipped stitch over

Pattern notes

This is a toe up, lace sock, with an afterthought heel.

Pattern

Toe

Using Judy's magic cast on, cast on 14 (15, 17) sts onto each of two needles, Rnd 1: Knit

Rnd 2: [K1, M1R, k to last st on needle, M1L, k1] twice.

Repeat these two rounds until you have 32 (35, 39) sts on each needle.

Foot

Size S only - slide 2 sts from one end of the second needle onto the first needle, M1L, k to end of rnd - 35 sts for front of sock, 30 sts for foot of sock

Size L only - You'll be working two knit stitches before and after the chart for the whole of the foot,

Rnd 1: First needle: K0 (0, 2), work Chart across foot section to last 0 (0, 2) sts, k0 (0, 2).

Second needle: Knit.

Work as set until, when tried on, your sock is almost at your ankle.

Afterthought heel prep

Needle 1: Work in pattern as set.

Needle 2: Knit the sts with waste yarn, leaving a 6 inch / 15.25 cm tail on either side of the sts, slide the sts back to the beginning of the needle, and reknit them with working yarn, knit across the remaining sts.

Leg

Rearrange your sts as follows:

Size S - Work in pattern as established over the first needle, k1, k2tog, k to last 3 sts, k2tog, k1 over the second needle - 35 sts on first needle, 28 sts on second needle.

Size M - no modifications.

Size L - slip the first two sts to the end of the second needle, work in patt across the first needle to the last 2 sts, slip them onto the second needle.

Continue working Chart across all sts until leg measures 6 (6.25, 6.5) inches / 15.25 (16.5, 17.75) cm.

Cuff

Rnd 1: *P1, k1, p1, k1, p1, k1, p1; repeat from * to end of rnd.

Repeat Rnd 1 for 2 (2.25, 2.5) inches / 5 (5.75, 6.25) cm.

Bind off using Jeny's Surprisingly stretchy bind off, or your favorite stretchy bind off techniques.

Afterthought heel

Working from one side of your heel prep rnd, carefully remove the waste yarn, a couple of sts at a time, placing the lower sts onto one needle, and the upper sts onto the second needle.

Make sure to count your sts, and ensure that you have the same number – if the number is off by one, work a k2tog at the beginning of the next rnd if necessary.

Rnd 1: [K1, ssk, k to 3 sts before end of needle, k2tog, k1] twice.

Rnd 2: Knit.

Work repeats of Rnds 1 and 2 until you have 13 (15, 17) sts remaining on each needle.

Break yarn, leaving a long tail.

Graft your sts together, using your

favorite grafting technique.

Finishing

Weave in ends securely. Block according to your ball band instructions.

Amenia

Required Skills

Working in the round

Increases / decreases

Twisted sts from chart

Sizes

S (M, L)

Finished Measurements

Circumference 7 (8.5, 9.5) inches / 17.75 (21.5, 22.75) cm – unstretched

Materials

A Hundred Ravens Patos (75% Merino, 25% nylon; 463yds / 425m per 4oz / 100g skein); color: Oceanus: 1 skein

US#2 / 2.75 mm circular needles

Cable needle

Stitch marker

Waste yarn for afterthought heel

Yarn needle

Gauge

32 sts x 40 rnds = 4 inches / 10 cm

Stitches and Techniques

k	knit
k2tog	knit 2 sts together
ktbl	knit through the back loop
p	purl
rnd(s)	round(s)
row(s)	row(s)
st(s)	stitch(es)
ssk	slip, slip, knit the two slipped sts together through the back loop
yo	yarn over
3st LT	slip 2 sts to cn, hold in front, k1, (p1, k1) from cn
3st RT	slip 1 st to cn, hold in back, k1, p1, (k1) from cn

Pattern notes

This sock is knitted from the top down, and has an afterthought heel.

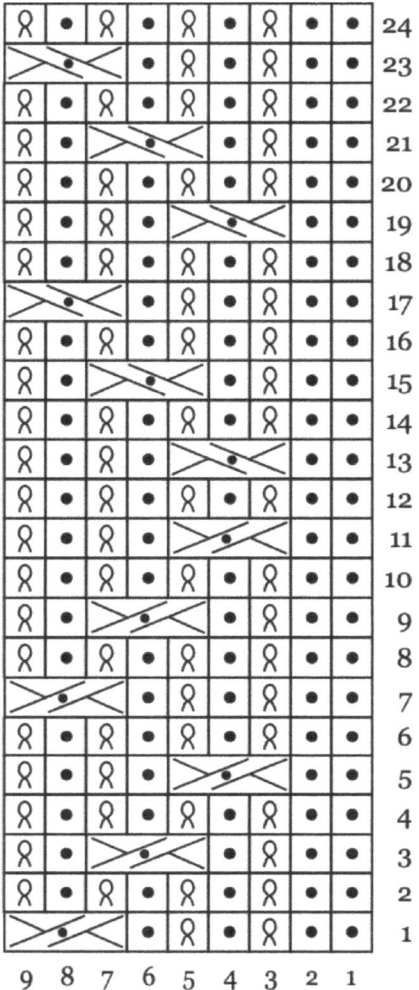

Pattern

Cuff

Using your favorite stretchy method, cast on 63 (72, 81) sts. Join to work in the round, and arrange your sts so that you have 36 (36, 45) sts on your first needle, and 27 (36, 36) sts on your second needle.

Rnd 1: *P2, [k1tbl, p1] three times, p1; repeat from * to end of rnd.

Repeat Rnd 1 for 1 (1.5, 1.5) inches / 2.5 (3.75) cm.

Leg

Work repeats of Chart across all sts for 6 (6.5, 7) inches / 15.25 (16.5, 17.75) cm.

Afterthought heel prep

Needle 1: Work in pattern as set.

Needle 2: Knit the sts with waste yarn, leaving a 6 inch / 15.25 cm tail on either side of the sts, slide the sts back to the beginning of the needle, and reknit them with working yarn, knit across the remaining sts

Foot

Work the Chart as set across the first needle, and work in St st across the second needle until your sock, when tried on, measures 2 (2.25, 2.5) inches / 5 (5.75, 6.25) cm shorter than your foot.

Toe

Size S - Slip 2 sts from the beginning of the rnd to end of second needle, k31, slip remaining sts onto second needle, knit across second needle to the last 2 sts, k2tog - 31 sts on each needle.

Size L - Slip the first 2 sts to second needle, k to last 4 sts of first needle, k2tog, slip last 2 sts to second needle, knit across second needle - 40 sts on each needle.

Rnd 1: [K1, ssk, k to last 3 sts on needle, k2tog, k1] twice.

Rnd 2: Knit.

Repeat Rnds 1 and 2 until you have 13 (16, 16) sts remaining.

Graft the toe together using your favorite seamless technique.

Afterthought heel

Working from one side of your heel prep rnd, carefully remove the waste yarn, a couple of sts at a time, placing the lower sts onto one needle, and the upper sts onto the second needle.

Make sure to count your sts, and ensure that you have the same number - if the number is off by one, work a k2tog at the beginning of the next rnd if necessary.

Rnd 1: [K1, ssk, k to last 3 sts on needle, k2tog, k1] twice.

Rnd 2: Knit.

Repeat Rnds 1 and 2 until you have 13 (16, 16) sts remaining.

Graft the heel together using your favorite seamless technique.

Finishing

Weave in ends. Block according to your ball band instructions.

Verbank

Required Skills

Working in the round

Increases / decreases

Simple lace from chart

Grafting

Sizes

S (M, L)

Finished Measurements

Circumference 7 (8.5, 9.5) inches / 17.75 (21.5, 22.75) cm - unstretched

Materials

Dirty Water Dyeworks Flecks (85% superwash Merino, 15% Donegal nep; 438yds / 400m per 4oz / 100g skein); color: Juniper: 1 skein

US#2 / 2.75 mm circular needles

Stitch marker

Yarn needle

Gauge 32 sts x 40 rnds = 4 inches / 10 cm - unstretched

Stitches and Techniques

CDD	(central double decrease) sl1, k2tog, psso
k	knit
k2tog	knit 2 sts together
ktbl	knit through the back loop
p	purl
rnd(s)	round(s)
row(s)	row(s)
st(s)	stitch(es)
ssk	slip, slip, knit the two slipped sts together through the back loop
yo	yarn over

Pattern Notes

This sock is worked from the top down, and has a gusseted heel

Pattern

Cuff

Using your favorite method, cast on 60 (72, 84) sts, and divide them equally over two needles. Join to work in the round, placing a marker to denote the beginning of the round.

Rnd 1: *K1tbl, p1; repeat from * to end of rnd.

Work repeats of Rnd 1 until your cuff measures 2 inches / 5 cm.

Leg

Work Chart across all sts for 6 (6.5, 7) inches / 15.25 (16.5, 17.75) cm.

Heel

Size S: K4, work 25 sts in pattern, k3 across first needle

Size M: Work 3 pattern repeats across first needle

Size L: K2, work 37 sts in patten, k1 across first needle

All sizes

*sl1, k1; repeat from * to end of rnd across second needle. Turn.

Working on second needle only:

Row 2: Sl1, p to end. Turn.

Row 3: *Sl1, k1; repeat from * to end of row. Turn.

Legend:
- ☐ Knit
- • Purl
- ඬ Ktbl
- ○ Yarn over
- ╱ K2tog
- ⋏ CDD

Row 4: Sl1, p to end. Turn.

Work a total of 17 (19, 21) repeats of Rows 3 and 4.

Heel turn

Row 1: Sl1, k14 (16, 18), ssk, k1. Turn.

Row 2: Sl1, p3, p2tog, p1. Turn.

Row 3: Sl1, k to one st before the gap, ssk, k1. Turn.

Row 4: Sl1, p to one st before the gap, p2tog, p1. Turn.

Repeat Rows 3 and 4 until all sts have been incorporated.

Gusset

Rnd 1: Knit across heel turn, pick up and knit 17 (19, 21) sts up the heel, work in pattern as established across the first needle, pick up and knit 17 (19, 21) sts along the remaining heel, knit to the end of the second needle.

Rnd 2: Work in pattern across first needle, k1, ssk, k to last 3 sts, k2tog, k1 across second needle.

Rnd 3: Work in pattern across first needle, knit across second needle.

Work repeats of Rnds 2 and 3 until you have 32 (36, 40) sts on each needle.

Leg

Work as set without shaping until, when tried on, your sock measures 2 (2.25, 2.5) inches / 5.75, 6.25) inches less than your foot.

Toe

Rnd 1: [K1, ssk, k to 3 sts before end of needle, k2tog, k1] twice.

Rnd 2: Knit.

Repeat Rnds 1 and 2 until you have 14 (16, 16) sts remaining on each needle.

Break yarn, leaving a long tail.

Graft sts together using your preferred seamless grafting technique.

Finishing

Weave in ends. Block according to your ball band instructions.

Wynkoop

Required Skills

Working in the round

Increases / decreases

Simple lace from chart

Grafting

Sizes

S (M, L)

Finished Measurements

Circumference 7 (8.5, 9.5) inches / 17.75 (21.5, 22.75) cm – unstretched

Materials

Into The Whirled Pakokku Sock (75% Superwash Merino / 25% Nylon; 460yds / 420m per 3.5oz / 110g skein); color: Cernunnos: 1 skein

US#2 / 2.75 mm circular needles

Stitch marker

Yarn needle

Gauge

32 sts x 40 rnds = 4 inches / 10 cm in stitch pattern, unstretched

Stitches and Techniques

- **k**   knit
- **k2tog**   knit 2 sts together
- **p**   purl
- **rnd(s)**   round(s)
- **row(s)**   row(s)
- **st(s)**   stitch(es)
- **ssk**   slip, slip, knit the two slipped sts together through the back loop
- **yo**   yarn over

Pattern Notes

This sock is worked from the cuff down, featuring lace across the leg, and top of foot, and has a gusseted heel.

Pattern

Cuff

Using your favorite method, cast on 60 (70, 80) sts, and divide them equally over two needles. Join to work in the round, placing a marker to denote the beginning of the round.

Rnd 1: *P1, k1, p2, k1; repeat from * to end of rnd.

Work repeats of Rnd 1 until your cuff measures 2 inches / 5 cm.

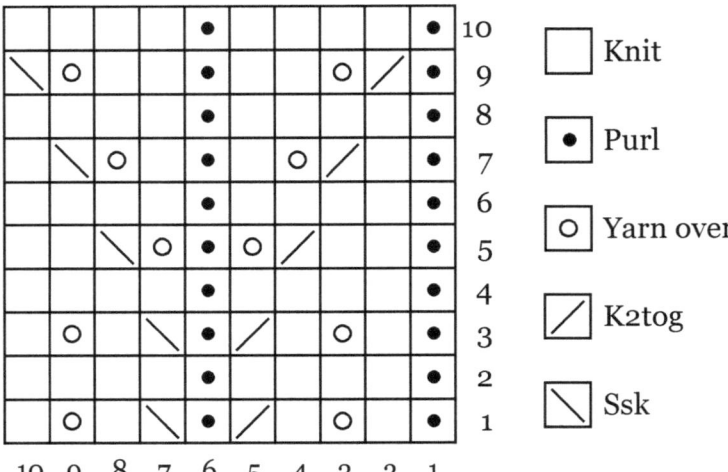

	Knit
•	Purl
○	Yarn over
╱	K2tog
╲	Ssk

Leg

Work Chart across all sts for 6 (6.5, 7) inches / 15.25 (16.5, 17.75) cm.

Heel

Size M only

Slip the last st of the second needle onto the first needle – 36 sts on first, 34 sts on second.

Rnd 1: Work in pattern as established across first needle, *sl1, k1; repeat from * to end of rnd across second needle. Turn.

Working on second needle only:

Row 2: Sl1, p to end. Turn.

Row 3: *Sl1, k1; repeat from * to end of row. Turn.

Row 4: Sl1, p to end. Turn.

Work a total of 17 (19, 21) repeats of Rows 3 and 4.

Heel turn

Row 1: Sl1, k15 (17, 20), ssk, k1. Turn.

Row 2: Sl1, p3, p2tog, p1. Turn.

Row 3: Sl1, k to one st before the gap, ssk, k1. Turn.

Row 4: Sl1, p to one st before the gap, p2tog, p1. Turn.

Repeat Rows 3 and 4 until all sts have been incorporated.

Gusset

Rnd 1: Knit across heel turn, pick up and knit 17 (19, 21) sts up the heel, work in pattern as established across the first needle, pick up and knit 17 (19, 21) sts along the remaining heel, knit to the end of the second needle.

Rnd 2: Work in pattern across first needle, k1, ssk, k to last 3 sts, k2tog, k1 across second needle.

Rnd 3: Work in pattern across first needle, knit across second needle.

Work repeats of Rnds 2 and 3 until you have 32 (36, 40) sts on each needle.

Leg

Work as set without shaping until, when tried on, your sock measures 2 (2.25, 2.5) inches / 5.75, 6.25) inches

less than your foot.

Toe

Rnd 1: [K1, ssk, k to 3 sts before end of needle, k2tog, k1] twice.

Rnd 2: Knit.

Repeat Rnds 1 and 2 until you have 14 (16, 16) sts remaining on each needle.

Break yarn, leaving a long tail.

Graft the sts together using your preferred grafting method.

Finishing

Weave in ends. Block according to your ball band instructions.

About CP

Cooperative Press was founded in 2007 by Shannon Okey, the author of this book and many others. She had been doing freelance acquisitions work, introducing authors with projects she believed in to editors at various publishers. And although working with traditional publishers can be very rewarding, there are some books that fly under their radar. They're too avant–garde, or the marketing department doesn't know how to sell them, or they don't think they'll sell 50,000 copies in a year.

5,000 or 50,000. Does the book matter to that 5,000? Then it should be published.

In 2009, Cooperative Press (cooperativepress. com) changed its name to reflect the relationships we have developed with authors working on books. We work together to put out the best quality books we can and share in the proceeds accordingly.

Thank you for supporting independent publishers and authors.

Cooperative Press can be found on

- Facebook: http://www.facebook.com/cooperativepress
- Instagram: http://www.instagram.com/cooperativepress
- Web/shop: http://cooperativepress.com

Thanks

Thanks to Sample knitters

Sarah Jo Burch

Marie Duquette

Cadence Journey-Rose Fingerholz

Stephanie Mcguckin

Candace Musmeci

Jessy Needles

Amy Ross

Kim Saar

Shannon Saar

Thanks to yarn companies

A Hundred Ravens

Dirty Dyewater

Dragonfly Fibers

Fiber Optic

Into The Whirled

Loop

Miss Babs

Neighborhood Fiber Company

Ross Farms

Andi Smith—without whom nothing would get done on my books, ever. Cheerleader, tech editor, ADHD whisperer and friend. You are the only partner I need to keep CP running no matter what life throws our way.

www.ingramcontent.com/pod-product-compliance
Lightning Source LLC
Chambersburg PA
CBHW042023180426
43199CB00039B/2929